OHIO DUI / OVI GUIDE

What You Need to Know Before Going to Court And Before Hiring a Lawyer For DUI / OVI in Ohio

Shawn Dominy, Attorney at Law

Rivers Edge Publishing, LLC

This guide is not legal advice. Although this guide is written by a lawyer and contains useful information about a legal issue, it is not legal advice, and reading it does not create an attorney-client relationship. The facts and circumstances of every OVI case are different. For a lawyer to give you legal advice, the lawyer needs to know the facts and circumstances of your particular case. Otherwise, it would be like a doctor performing a medical procedure without knowing your symptoms and medical history. If you want legal advice for your specific case, you should hire a lawyer with expertise in the area of OVI defense.

The characters and events portrayed in this book are fictitious. Any similarity to real persons, living or dead, is coincidental and not intended by the author.

ISBN-978-1-7368732-0-5

Cover design by: Shawn R. Dominy
Author Photo by: Klatte Photography

Printed in the United States of America

CONTENTS

WHY THIS GUIDE WAS WRITTEN

People charged with OVI have a lot of questions. Being charged with OVI is stressful, and nobody is prepared for it to happen. When it does, a deluge of thoughts overflow your mind.

- What exactly is an OVI?
- What are the consequences if I'm found guilty of OVI?
- Why did the officer conclude I was under the influence?
- What happens at the court appearances?
- Is there any chance of avoiding an OVI conviction?
- Should I hire a lawyer?
- Does it make a difference which lawyer I hire?
- How can I find a good OVI lawyer?

I wrote this guide to answer those questions. I am a DUI/OVI lawyer and the founder of the Dominy Law Firm in Columbus, Ohio. With over two decades of helping people charged with OVI, I know how empowering it has been for my clients to receive answers to their questions. Reading the information in this guide is a great way to have your questions answered.

After being charged with OVI, the best thing you can do is educate yourself about OVI cases and OVI lawyers. First, educating yourself will give you an accurate understanding of your situation, which will hopefully reduce the anxiety you're experiencing. Second, learning more will help you avoid the mistakes commonly made in OVI cases. Third, having this information will help you determine whether you will hire a lawyer. If you choose to hire a lawyer, this guide will assist you in selecting a good lawyer to defend you.

There is a lot of misinformation about OVI cases and OVI lawyers. Television, movies, and 'urban legends' are full of misunderstandings. Lawyer advertising is not very helpful at clarifying these misunderstandings. All of the websites for 'DUI lawyers' look about the same, but the reality is all lawyers are not the same. Some have more expertise than others, some get better results than others, and some provide better customer service than others. The problem is it's hard to tell which ones.

This guide will help. In privacy and comfort, you can have your questions answered by reading this guide. *Part One* explains OVI and its consequences, to give you a better understanding of the offense and what you're facing if you're found guilty. *Part Two* discusses evidence in OVI cases, including what officers are trained to observe and the procedures officers are expected to follow. *Part Three* addresses the defenses used in OVI cases to help improve case outcomes. *Part Fou*r describes the court process, so you will know what to expect at court appearances.

Part Five provides a framework for evaluating whether you want to plead guilty or fight the OVI, as well as whether you want to hire a lawyer. If you decide to hire a lawyer, *Part Five* also identifies resources for researching lawyers, a list of qualifications to look for in OVI lawyers, and several questions to ask before hiring a lawyer.

My goal in writing this guide is to provide you with the valuable information you should have before going to court and before hiring a lawyer for an OVI in Ohio. My hope is that, by reading this guide, you will understand the consequences, the evidence, the court process, and the differences among lawyers. With that knowledge, you can make well-informed decisions about how to handle your OVI case.

Shawn Dominy, Attorney at Law

THIS GUIDE IS NOT LEGAL ADVICE

Although this guide is written by a lawyer and contains

useful information about a legal issue, it is not legal advice, and reading it does not create an attorney-client relationship. The facts and circumstances of every OVI case are different. For a lawyer to give you legal advice, the lawyer needs to know the facts and circumstances of your particular case. Otherwise, it would be like a doctor performing a medical procedure without knowing your symptoms and medical history. If you want legal advice for your specific case, you should hire a lawyer with expertise in the area of OVI defense.

PART ONE: OVI AND ITS CONSEQUENCES

WHAT IS OVI?

Drunk driving is known by many acronyms, and those acronyms vary from state-to-state. Many states call it DUI, some refer to it as DWI, and others call it OMVI. In Ohio, it's called **OVI**, which stands for **O**perating a **V**ehicle under the **I**nfluence of alcohol and/or drugs. Ohio does not have the M from OMVI (for Motorized) because, in Ohio, the vehicle does not have to be motorized: you can be charged with OVI on your bicycle! The important question is this: what does the prosecution have to prove for you to be found guilty of OVI?

TYPES OF OVI CHARGES

There are two general types of OVI charges, which means there are two general ways a prosecutor can try to prove your guilt: OVI "impaired"; and (2) OVI "per se".

O.V.I. "Impaired". The prosecution must prove you *operated a vehicle **'under the influence'** of alcohol and/or drugs*. You are considered 'under the influence' if the alcohol or drug affected your nervous system, brain, or muscles to noticeably impair your actions, reactions, or mental processes - which *impaired* your ability to operate a vehicle. For the "impaired" charge, the level of alcohol or drugs does not matter. All that matters is the alcohol or drugs impaired your ability to drive.

OVI "Per Se". The prosecution must prove you *operated a vehicle with a **prohibited concentration** of alcohol or drugs in your blood, breath, or urine*. For the "per se" charge, it does not matter whether the alcohol or drug was impairing your ability to drive. All that matters is you had a prohibited concentration of alcohol or drugs in your system -you were over the 'legal limit'- when you operated the vehicle. The prohibited concentrations for alcohol and drugs are listed in the table below.

The Traffic Ticket. If you do *not* take a breath/blood/urine test, or if the test result is *not* over the 'legal limit', you are charged only with OVI "impaired". If you take a breath/blood/urine test and the test result *is* over the 'legal limit', you are typically charged with both OVI "impaired" and OVI "per se".

Prohibited Concentrations: OVI "Per Se"

Substance	Blood	Urine	Breath
Alcohol	.080 %	.110 %	.080 %
Amphetamine / Methamphetamine	100 ng	500 ng	
Cocaine	50 ng	150 ng	
Heroin	50 ng	2,000 ng	
Heroin Metabolite	10 ng	10 ng	
L.S.D.	10 ng	25 ng	
Marijuana	2 ng	10 ng	
Marijuana Metabolite	50 ng	35 ng	
MJ Metabolite & Under the Influence	5 ng	15 ng	

OVI-"Drugged Driving". Ohio law makes it illegal to operate a vehicle "under the influence of alcohol, a drug of abuse, or a combination of them". This OVI "impaired" offense applies to illegal drugs, marijuana, and prescription medications. For some drugs, there is also an OVI "per se" offense based on a prohibited level of the drug (summarized in the chart above).

OVI-Repeat Offenses. For each conviction within ten years, the mandatory penalties increase. The penalties are summarized in the section below titled, "Consequences of an OVI Conviction".

OVI-"Test Refusal with Prior Conviction". The prosecution must prove you committed the offense of OVI, you had a prior OVI conviction within the last 20 years, and you refused a blood/breath/urine test. A conviction for this offense doubles the minimum mandatory jail term.

OVI-Underage. Individuals under 21 may be charged with OVI "impaired" and OVI "per se". In addition, a driver under 21 with a blood alcohol concentration of .020 to .079 may be charged with OVUAC: Operating a Vehicle after Under Age Consumption.

BUI-Boating Under the Influence: The prosecution must prove you operated a boat (or other vessel) under the influence of alcohol and/or drugs ("impaired") or with a prohibited concentration of alcohol and/or drugs ("per se"). The 'legal limits' for operating a boat are the same as those for operating a vehicle.

CONSEQUENCES OF AN OVI CONVICTION

If you are convicted of OVI, there are mandatory minimum sentences a judge *must* impose, and there is a broad range of punishments a judge *may* impose. The punishment imposed by the court will include incarceration, a license suspension, a fine, court costs, and points on your driver's license. The punishment may also include yellow license plates, an ignition interlock device, vehicle immobilization or forfeiture, continuous alcohol monitoring, alcohol/drug treatment, and probation.

The minimum mandatory sentences and the maximum possible sentences increase based upon the number of prior OVI convictions within the last ten years and the last 20 years. The following table summarizes the potential OVI sentences in Ohio.

Potential Sentences for OVI in Ohio

Offense Number	Jail Term	Fine & Costs	License Suspension	Time w/o Privileges	Immobilize or Forfeit Car?	Yellow Plates & Interlock
First	3 days to 6 months	$375 to $1,075	1 year to 3 years	15 days	No	Maybe
Second	10 days to 6 months	$525 to $1,625	1 year to 7 years	45 days	90 days	Yes
Third	30 days to 12 months	$850 to $2,750	2 years to 12 years	180 days	Forfeiture	Yes
Felony (First)	60 days to 30 months	$1,350 - $10,500	3 years to Life	3 years	Forfeiture	Yes
Felony (Second)	60 days to 5 years	$1,350 - $10,500	3 years to Life	3 years	Forfeiture	Yes

Notes about this table: First, if the conviction is for a "high test" (blood alcohol concentration of .170 or higher) or for a "test refusal with prior conviction" (in the last 20 years), the minimum mandatory jail term is doubled. Second, the table is a very simplified summary of OVI sentencing at the time this guide was written; there are variations to these sentences. Third, OVI sentencing is subject to change at any time by the Ohio legislature.

Secondary Consequences. In addition to the punishment imposed by the court, there are also secondary consequences of an OVI conviction. A conviction is a permanent public record which cannot be sealed or expunged. A conviction will substantially increase premiums for auto insurance and may result in increased premiums for life insurance and health insurance. A conviction may also affect the following:

*Current and prospective employment

*Eligibility to drive a company vehicle

*Commercial Driver License

*Professional license

*Educational and athletic eligibility

*Military acceptance or discipline

*Security clearances
*Loan applications
*Ability to transport children
*Immigration status
*Travel to other countries
*Reputation

Part One has explained OVI charges and their consequences. Before you incur any of those consequences, the evidence must first prove you are guilty of OVI. Evidence for OVI cases is discussed in *Part Two*.

The Real (average) Cost of an OVI Conviction

Towing and storage of vehicle	$ 150
Fine and court costs	$ 600
License reinstatement fee	$ 475
Driver intervention program	$ 450
Ignition interlock device	$ 600
Insurance premium increase for three years	$5,350
Loss of income	Varies
Record/reputation	Priceless

ADMINISTRATIVE LICENSE SUSPENSIONS

License suspensions in OVI cases can be confusing. There are two different types of suspensions:

(1) if you refuse the test or test over the limit, an *Administrative License Suspension* (ALS) is immediately imposed by the Ohio Bureau of Motor Vehicles (BMV)

(2) if you are found guilty of OVI, a *Court Suspension* is imposed by the judge.

For both types of suspensions, the court may grant limited driving privileges. There is, however, a waiting period ("hard time") during which the court cannot grant limited driving privileges.

The length of the ALS, and the waiting period for driving privileges, depends on whether you refused to take the test or tested 'over the limit', as well as the number of prior OVI convictions and test refusals on your record. The following tables summarize Administrative License Suspensions in Ohio:

ALS for Test Refusal

Refusals/Convictions in the last 10 Years	Length of Suspension	Waiting Period for Driving Privileges
No priors	One year	30 days
One prior	Two years	90 days
Two priors	Three years	One year
Three priors	Five years	Three years

ALS for Test 'Over the Limit'

Refusals/Convictions in the last 10 Years	Length of Suspension	Waiting Period for Driving Privileges
No priors	90 days	15 days
One prior	One year	45 days
Two priors	Two years	180 days
Three priors	Three years	Three years

Administrative License Suspensions are part of Ohio's 'implied consent' law. That law states any driver who operates a vehicle in the state of Ohio implicitly consents to take a blood/breath/urine test for alcohol and/or drugs if the driver is arrested for OVI. 'Implied consent' also applies to any driver who is unconscious or otherwise in a condition rendering the person incapable of refusing.

A driver license is considered property, and no person can be deprived of property without due process of law. Accordingly, if your license is being suspended, you have the right to due process of law. That means the ALS is only valid if the officer followed the procedures required by Ohio law. Officers do not always follow the required procedures.

Your right to due process also means you must be given notice of the suspension and an opportunity to appeal the suspension. There are two ways to challenge the ALS:

1. Motion Appealing the ALS
2. Motion to Terminate the ALS

The grounds for the motion *appealing* the ALS are found in Ohio Revised Code section 4511.197. The bases for the motion to *terminate* the ALS are found in Ohio Revised Code section 4511.192. The most common attacks on the ALS are discussed later, in the section for *Defenses to the Administrative License Suspension.*

Case Example

In a recent case of ours, the officer gave our client an ALS notice but did not complete the section where the officer states the reasons for asking our client to take a test. Ohio law requires the officer to give the defendant a 'completed' form, and the form given to our client was not 'completed'. We appealed, and the ALS was terminated at the arraignment.

PART TWO: EVIDENCE IN OVI CASES

WHAT OFFICERS LOOK FOR WHEN YOU ARE DRIVING

Officers undergo training in OVI detection and investigation. That training divides the OVI investigation into three phases, and the first phase is the 'Vehicle In Motion' phase. Officers are taught to look for certain clues that the driver of a vehicle in motion is under the influence. Those clues include:

- Weaving, driving outside the marked lane, making wide turns
- Striking or nearly striking objects
- Problems stopping, erratic speed changes
- Responding slowly to traffic signals, driving without headlights
- Unsafe lane changes, improper turns, driving recklessly

Officers must have a legal justification to stop your car. Your attorney should obtain the cruiser video to see if the officer had a valid reason to stop you. If the judge concludes the stop was not justified, any evidence obtained after the stop is excluded. Even if the judge concludes the stop was justified, the video may show the officer did not observe 'clues' from the 'Vehicle In Motion' phase. The absence of those clues can be used in court to show you were not under the influence.

If you were involved in an accident, the officer likely did not observe the vehicle in motion. That means there were no clues from that phase of the investigation. However, that also means the officer did not make a traffic stop and was justified to interact with you as part of the accident investigation. The prosecutor may argue the accident is evidence you were under the influence.

Case Examples

In one case, our client was stopped for a Marked Lanes violation, but the cruiser video showed our client only touched the line and didn't go over it: OVI dismissed. In another case, the officer claimed our client's headlights weren't on. The cruiser video was inconclusive, and we made our own video showing how the headlights worked for our client's car. Before a hearing on the issue, the prosecutor reduced the OVI to a minor offense with no license suspension and no jail time.

WHAT OFFICERS LOOK FOR WHEN THEY STOP YOU AND TALK WITH YOU

In addition to needing a justification to stop you, officers also need a valid reason to further detain you (get you out of the car) for field sobriety tests. When the cruiser lights come on, the officer will take note of any delay in responding to the cruiser lights and whether you had difficulty stopping your vehicle safely.

After the stop begins the 'Personal Contact' phase of the OVI investigation. During this phase, the officer is looking for evidence you are under the influence, such as:

- Odor of alcohol, 'cover up' odors, bloodshot/glassy eyes
- Slurred speech, admission of drinking, inconsistent responses
- Soiled clothing, alcohol containers, drug paraphernalia
- Problems with vehicle controls
- Lack of coordination getting your license and insurance card

When you are getting your license and insurance card, the officer purposely asks you questions to see if you have difficulty dividing your attention between retrieving the documents and answering the officer's questions. Driving is a 'divided attention' skill, so difficulty dividing your attention is circumstantial evidence you are driving under the influence. The officer is trying to decide whether to remove you from the vehicle for field sobriety tests because getting you out of the vehicle is a seizure of your person which must be justified.

Your lawyer should review the evidence closely to determine whether the officer was justified in further detaining you to administer tests. If the evidence did not justify further detention, any evidence obtained after that detention should be thrown out.

I have had many cases in which the stop was justified but the OVI was dismissed or reduced because the justification for further detention was questionable. Even if the judge concludes further detention was justified, the evidence may show the officer did not observe many 'clues' they are trained to look for. The absence of those 'clues' can be used in court to show you were not under the influence.

FIELD SOBRIETY TESTS

After an officer removes you from your vehicle, the officer almost always administers field sobriety tests. You are not required to take those tests, and there are no penalties for declining the tests. Officers do not tell people this, so nearly everybody takes them.

The *three standardized field sobriety tests* are designed to help the officer decide whether to charge you with OVI. The tests also are used by the prosecution to argue your performance on the tests is circumstantial evidence that you were under the influence or 'over the limit'.

Horizontal Gaze Nystagmus Test. The officer has you follow a pen or a finger with your eyes. During this test, the officer is looking for an involuntary jerking of the eyeball (nystagmus) because studies show that alcohol and some drugs increase the presence of nystagmus. During this six-part test, the officer scores a "clue" each time nystagmus is observed. There are six possible "clues", and the presence of four or more "clues" suggests your blood alcohol content is .08 or higher.

Walk And Turn Test. The officer instructs you to stand on a line, walk nine heel-to-toe steps down the line, turn around, and walk nine heel-to-toe steps back. As you perform the test, the officer looks for "clues". There are eight possible "clues", and the presence of two or more "clues" indicates a probability that your blood alcohol content is .08 or higher. The eight "clues" are:

- lose your balance during the instructions
- start too early
- fail to touch heel-to-toe

- stop walking
- step off the line
- raise your arms for balance
- turn improperly
- take an incorrect number of steps

One Leg Stand Test. The officer instructs you to raise one foot approximately six inches off the ground, stand on the other leg with your arms at your sides, and count aloud for 30 seconds. As you perform the test, the officer scores "clues". There are four possible “clues”, and the presence of two or more “clues” indicates a probability that your blood alcohol content is .08 or higher. The four clues are:

- sway
- use your arms for balance
- hop
- put your foot down

Non-Standardized Tests. In addition to the three standardized field sobriety tests, some officers also administer non-standardized tests, such as counting backward, reciting part of the alphabet, and touching your nose with your eyes closed and your head tilted back. These tests have no standardized procedure, and no studies show a correlation between these tests and being under the influence or ‘over the limit’.

Your attorney should scrutinize the field sobriety tests. If your attorney has training in field sobriety testing, he or she can review the cruiser video and cross-examine the officer to determine if the officer made mistakes administering the tests. I have had many cross-examinations reveal the officer made mistakes, which resulted in the tests being thrown out. Even if the tests are not thrown out, effective cross-examination of the officer can show why the tests really do not measure intoxication.

Are Field Sobriety Tests Fair?

When officers administer field sobriety tests, they do not tell subjects what "clues" will be scored, and they do not give subjects an opportunity to practice. What other tests do people take where they are not told what is being graded and are not permitted to study? If standing on one leg and walking heel-to-toe can predict driving ability, why aren't those tests part of the driver's license examination?

HOW OFFICERS DECIDE IF YOU WILL BE CHARGED WITH OVI

After the field sobriety tests, the officer decides whether you are going to be charged with OVI. If you are going to be charged, the officer typically handcuffs you and puts you in the cruiser.

Some people believe they were not 'arrested because they were not taken to a police station or jail. An 'arrest actually occurs when the officer decides you are going to be charged with OVI and detains you (usually, but not always, in handcuffs) to give you the ticket. To justify arresting you, the officer must have probable cause to believe you operated a vehicle under the influence or 'over the limit'.

The decision to arrest you is supposed to be based upon the 'totality of the circumstances'. In addition to considering all the evidence indicating you *are* under the influence, the officer should also consider all the evidence indicating you are *not* under the influence. The evidence includes everything the officer observes while you are driving, when you stop, while speaking with you, and when the field sobriety tests are administered.

Your lawyer should look closely at the circumstances leading to the arrest. If the arrest was not justified by probable cause, any evidence obtained after the arrest is excluded, including any blood/breath/urine tests and any statements you made to the officer. When evidence is excluded due to lack of probable cause, the OVI charge is often dismissed or reduced.

What if I Barely Open my Window and Refuse to Get Out?

If you do this, the officer will have to decide whether to arrest you. On one hand, if the officer arrests you, the officer will not have field sobriety tests as evidence. On the other hand, the officer may still have enough evidence to arrest you from the 'Vehicle In Motion' phase and the 'Personal Contact' phase. When the prosecutor reads a police report indicating the driver barely opened the window and refused to get out of the car, the prosecutor is going to be less inclined than usual to offer a favorable plea agreement.

QUESTIONING BY OFFICERS AND THE MIRANDA MYTH

The most common misunderstanding in OVI cases is probably the impact of *Miranda* warnings. Television and movies would have us believe the officer's failure to issue *Miranda* warnings means the whole case is thrown out.

If only it were that easy....

During the OVI investigation, the officer likely asked you questions. Officers typically ask where you have been, how much alcohol or drugs you consumed, what type of drinks or drugs you ingested, over what period of time you consumed the alcohol or drugs, and how much you ate. Officers also may ask if you are under the influence or have you rate your intoxication on a scale of one to ten. If you make statements that incriminate you (e.g., "I drank 19 beers"), the prosecution would like to use those statements against you in court.

The principle from the Miranda case is this: if you are in custody and the officer does not give you *Miranda* warnings, any statements you make while in custody cannot be used against you at trial. That is the impact of *Miranda*. The statements are thrown out, but not the entire case.

When you are 'in custody' is a gray area. An Ohio Supreme Court case states you do not have to be formally arrested to be 'in custody'. When the situation changes from a routine traffic stop to an OVI investigation, you may be 'in custody'.

Your attorney should investigate the circumstances surrounding any statements you made to the police. If you made incriminating statements while you were 'in custody' and the officer did not issue *Miranda* warnings, your attorney should file a motion to suppress (throw out) those statements.

Case Example

Our client drove his motorcycle, with his girlfriend on the back, and parked in the driveway to a city building. A city employee saw my client and his girlfriend but could not say who was driving. While answering an officer's questions, our client made incriminating statements. The prosecutor needed the statements to get a conviction. However, the officer did not issue Miranda warnings, so the statements were going to be excluded. Our client's third OVI within ten years was reduced to a non-moving violation.

TESTING BLOOD/ BREATH/URINE TO MEASURE ALCOHOL AND DRUG LEVELS

When too much alcohol, or another drug, gets to your brain, it impairs abilities necessary for driving. Those abilities include vision, coordination, and reactions. Although the same amount of alcohol or drugs may have very different effects on different people, the 'legal limit' for everyone is the same.

Ohio's OVI 'per se' laws make it illegal to operate a vehicle with a prohibited amount of alcohol or drugs. Therefore, law enforcement must have a way to measure the amount of alcohol and drugs in a person's system. The most accurate measurement probably would be obtained by testing brain tissue, but even 'tough on crime' politicians would not recommend that method. In Ohio, alcohol and drug levels are measured in blood, breath, and urine.

Blood tests are considered to be the most accurate tests because they 'directly' measure the level of alcohol and drugs in your blood. In Ohio, there are two types of blood tests: (1) crime lab tests, and (2) hospital tests. Crime lab blood tests do not require expert testimony but must comply with regulations by the Ohio Department of Health to be admissible. Hospital blood tests do not need to comply with those regulations but do require expert testimony to make them admissible.

Blood tests can be done against your will. An officer may have your blood forcibly drawn if the officer obtains a search warrant, or if there are 'exigent circumstances': a compelling need for the blood and no time to secure a warrant. For cases involving blood tests, there are many issues for your lawyer to explore, including the manner in which the blood is drawn, collected, sealed, labeled, stored, transported, and tested. Problems in any of those areas can lead to the blood test being thrown out or having its accuracy doubted.

Breath tests indirectly measure blood alcohol content. Alcohol in your blood makes its way into your lungs and is expired when you exhale. Rather than go through the hassle of drawing your blood, officers can more conveniently measure the alcohol in your breath by having you blow into a machine.

For the breath test to be admissible in court, it must be conducted using an approved machine, and the machine must be maintained in compliance with a long list of regulations. Your lawyer should check the records for the breath-testing machine to determine if the police department failed to comply with any of those regulations. If the police department did not substantially comply with the regulations, the breath test is thrown out. Your lawyer also should explore any possible explanations for why the machine did not produce an accurate result in your test.

Urine tests, like breath tests, indirectly measure blood alcohol levels. Unlike breath tests, urine tests also measure drug levels. The concentration of alcohol or drugs in your urine is not the same as the concentration in your blood, so the alcohol and drug limits are different for urine. Most states do not use urine tests as evidence because alcohol or drugs may remain in urine long after they have dissipated from the blood and are no longer affecting your ability to drive. Nevertheless, Ohio uses urine testing in OVI cases.

For a urine test to be admissible in court, the test must be conducted in compliance with Ohio regulations. If the urine sample was not collected, handled, transported, tested, and stored in compliance with those regulations, the test is thrown out. If the urine test is not thrown out, you may still introduce evidence to show why the result was not accurate.

Breath Testing in Ohio

Ohio is unique in its approach to the litigation of breath test cases. In the 1984 case of State v. Vega, the Ohio Supreme Court held that a defendant may not make a general attack on the reliability and validity of the breath-testing machine. Some courts interpret Vega to prohibit any attack.

In the 2013 case of State v. Lancaster, an Ohio Court held that a defendant may attack the reliability of the specific testing procedure and the particular equipment used for the breath test. The judge concluded that, although a breath-testing machine is presumed to be reliable, the defense proved that the Intoxilyzer 8000 machines used in those cases are not reliable. As a result, tests on those particular machines are not admissible as evidence. I was defense counsel in this case, and you can read more about the case on the Dominy Law Firm blog

•

Should I Take the Test?

When a driver is arrested for OVI in Ohio, the driver is asked to submit to a breath/blood/urine test. Some lawyers advise everyone to refuse the test. That is not always good advice. Before taking or refusing a test, the following possible outcomes should be considered:

If you *take* the test and the result is *over* the prohibited amount:

(a) your license will be suspended for 90 days (or longer if you have prior OVI convictions or test refusals)

(b) you will be charged with OVI "per se" and OVI "impaired"

(c) the prosecution will use the results of the test against you in court.

If you *take* the test and the result is *under* the prohibited amount:

(a) your license will not be suspended

(b) you will not be charged with OVI "per se" – only OVI "impaired"

(b) the results of the test will not be damaging in court

If you *refuse* the test:

(a) your license will be suspended for one year (or longer if you have prior OVI convictions or test refusals)

(b) you will not be charged with OVI "per se" – only OVI "impaired"

(b) the prosecution will not have test results to use against you in court.

If you *refuse* the test, in some circumstances, you may have blood drawn involuntarily. This can be the worst of both worlds if the test result is 'over the limit': your license is suspended for refusing the test, and the prosecution will use the blood test results in court.

For some people, there is additional punishment for refusing the breath/blood/urine test. If you have a prior OVI conviction within 20 years, refusal of the test a separate offense with additional consequences. If you are a commercial driver with a CDL, you face additional sanctions for refusing the test. If you are on probation for OVI, refusing is typically a violation of probation.

DRUG RECOGNITION EVALUATIONS

If a law enforcement officer suspects a driver is under the influence of drugs, the officer may administer a drug recognition evaluation. Unlike the field sobriety tests, which are conducted *before* a driver is arrested, a drug recognition evaluation is administered *after* the driver's arrest. The purposes of the evaluation are to determine whether the driver is under the influence of a drug and predict what class of drug is causing the driver's impairment.

The evaluations must conducted by an officer who is certified as a Drug Recognition Evaluator, also called a Drug Recognition Expert (DRE). To become a DRE, an officer must complete the 72-hour 'Drug Examination and Classification Program'. The DRE program has been used in Ohio since the 1990s, but there are relatively few certified DREs in Ohio, so arresting officers often call-in a DRE to perform a drug recognition evaluation.

The drug recognition evaluation, typically administered at a police station, is a 12-step assessment. Some of the steps in the evaluation repeat tests which were likely performed before the arrest. The 12 steps are:

1. Breath Alcohol Test
2. Interview of the Arresting Officer
3. Preliminary Examination and First Pulse
4. Eye Examination: Horizontal Gaze Nystagmus, Vertical Nystagmus, and Lack Of Convergence
5. Divided Attention Tests: Modified Romberg, Walk And Turn, One Leg Stand, Finger-To-Nose

6. Vital Signs and Second Pulse
7. Pupil Size: reaction to light and rebound dilation
8. Muscle Tone
9. Injection Sites and Third Pulse
10. Subject's Statements and Other Observations
11. Analysis and Opinions of the Evaluator
12. Toxicological Examination: blood and/or urine

The evaluations are subject to confirmation bias, some components of the evaluation are not related to drug impairment, and the protocol was not subjected to critical peer review. Subsequent validation studies show the evaluations are ineffective, resulting in false-positives and false-negatives.

PART THREE: DEFENSES IN OVI CASES

DEFENSES TO OVI GENERALLY

Defenses in Ohio OVI cases are usually not the traditional criminal law defenses. The traditional criminal defenses include alibi, duress, entrapment, necessity, etc. Those defenses are rarely used in OVI cases.

Instead, the 'defenses' in OVI cases are methods of excluding evidence and strategies for demonstrating the remaining evidence does not prove guilt. What defenses are employed in a case depends on the type of charge. As discussed above, there are two general types of OVI charges: OVI 'impaired' and OVI 'per se'.

The lawyers at the Dominy Law Firm created a list of '*The Top 100 Ohio DUI / OVI Defenses*'©. That list does not contain every possible defense; just the top 100. Of those 100 defenses, 50 are related to the charge of OVI 'impaired', and 50 are related to the charge of OVI 'per se'. The list also includes a summary of the *Top 10 Defenses to the Administrative License Suspension*.

DEFENSES TO OVI 'IMPAIRED'

For the charge of OVI 'impaired', the prosecution must prove you operated a vehicle 'under the influence' of alcohol and/or drugs. The level of alcohol or drugs does not matter. All that matters is the alcohol or drugs impaired your ability to drive.

Proving the OVI 'Impaired' charge relies heavily on observations of witnesses, primarily police officers. The proof comes from the cumulative effect of the individual pieces of evidence, like ingredients in a recipe (e.g., unsafe driving, slurred speech, poor performance on sobriety tests, etc.). The defenses are designed to show there are incorrect or missing ingredients. Not every case involves every defense: we use only the defenses applicable to that particular case.

Here are the top 50 defenses for the charge of OVI 'impaired':

1. Driving: 'clues' of impaired driving not present while vehicle is in motion
2. Driving: 'clues' observed by officer are unrelated to driving under the influence
3. Driving: no proof of 'operation' of the vehicle
4. Driving: no problems with stopping sequence
5. Traffic stop not justified: no traffic violation committed
6. Traffic stop not justified: insufficient informant tip
7. Traffic stop not justified: unreasonable mistake of fact/law by officer
8. Accident: not at fault, poor accident investigation
9. Accident: alcohol or drugs consumed after accident

10. Sobriety checkpoint unlawful
11. Interaction with officer: no odor of alcohol
12. Interaction with officer: no slurred speech
13. Interaction with officer: no glassy/bloodshot eyes
14. Interaction with officer: no admission of consuming alcohol or drugs
15. Interaction with officer: no problem with mental faculties
16. Interaction with officer: no problem with physical coordination
17. Interaction with officer: no problem with divided attention
18. No evidence of alcohol or drugs/drug paraphernalia in vehicle
19. Detention for DUI/OVI investigation not justified
20. Field sobriety tests: not admissible due to lack of compliance with training manual
21. Field sobriety tests: not reliable due to faulty administration
22. Field sobriety tests: good performance from common sense perspective despite observation of technical 'clues'
23. Field sobriety tests: unrelated to impaired driving ability
24. Field sobriety tests: medical condition affected ability to perform tests
25. Field sobriety tests: non-standardized tests have no correlation with intoxication
26. Field sobriety tests: non-standardized tests inadmissible under rules of evidence
27. Drug recognition evaluations: 12-steps not properly implemented
28. Drug recognition evaluations: failure to comply with certification requirement
29. Drug recognition evaluations: components unrelated to driving impairment
30. No problems with balance
31. No problems with coordination
32. No problems following instructions
33. Arrest unlawful: officer did not have probable cause to believe driver was under the influence
34. Arrest unlawful: officer outside jurisdiction

35. Statements made to officer inadmissible due to lack of *Miranda* warnings
36. Statements made to officer inaccurately reported or taken out of context
37. Fatigue has symptoms which can be mistaken for intoxication
38. Medical conditions may have symptoms which can be mistaken for intoxication
39. Ambien use negates the *actus reus* requirement; the act of driving is involuntary
40. Confirmation bias: officer jumped to conclusion and looked for evidence to confirm conclusion
41. Officer discounted evidence inconsistent with intoxication
42. Officer under pressure to make OVI arrests
43. Refusal of chemical test: no advice or improper advice given regarding consequences of refusing test
44. Refusal of chemical test: no notification of right to appeal or independent chemical test
45. Refusal of chemical test: officer's claim of refusal inaccurate
46. Refusal of chemical test: inability to take test is not a refusal
47. Refusal of chemical test: enhancement of penalty improper because prior OVI convictions 'invalid'
48. Discovery: evidence from prosecutor not disclosed to defense attorney
49. Discovery: evidence destroyed after requested by defense
50. Speedy trial rights violated

DEFENSES TO OVI 'PER SE'

For the charge of OVI 'per se', the prosecution must prove you operated a vehicle with a prohibited concentration of alcohol or drugs in your blood, breath, or urine. It does not matter whether the alcohol or drug was impairing your ability to drive. All that matters is you had a prohibited concentration of alcohol or drugs in your system (you were over the 'legal limit') when you operated the vehicle.

To prove your alcohol and/or drug level was 'over the limit', the prosecution will introduce the results of a breath test, blood test, or urine test. The defenses to OVI 'per se' generally aim to exclude the test results from evidence or explain why the test results were inaccurate.

Here are the top 50 defenses for the charge of OVI 'per se':

Breath Tests

1. Test result does not prove BAC was 'over the limit' at the time of operating the vehicle due to rising BAC
2. Breath temperature was not measured, and breath temperature affected test result
3. Driver's breathing pattern affected test result
4. Cell phone in area of breath test caused radio frequency interference
5. Breath-testing machine plugged into outlet with other electrical devices
6. Driver had foreign substance in mouth at time of breath test
7. Medical condition affected accuracy of test
8. Ambient air contained alcohol which inflated test result
9. Breath-testing machine not properly maintained

10. Officer did not conduct 20-minute observation period before test
11. Invalid sample not followed by 20-minute observation period
12. Records for breath-testing machine not maintained for prescribed period
13. Instrument check not performed every seven days
14. Instrument check did not yield valid result
15. Radio frequency interference check not performed every seven days
16. Instrument check solution used beyond expiration date
17. Instrument check solution not refrigerated when not in use
18. Instrument check solution container not retained for prescribed period
19. Breath test operator did not have valid permit
20. Breath-testing machine senior operator for maintenance did not have valid permit
21. Breath-testing machine not in proper working order

Blood & Urine Tests

22. No search warrant and no exception to search warrant requirement
23. Defective search warrant
24. Procedure manual for test not on file in analytical testing area
25. Procedures used by laboratory not scientifically valid
26. Procedures for analytical testing not followed
27. Technique used for testing not approved by Ohio Department of Health
28. Instrument(s) used for testing were not calibrated daily
29. Instrument(s) used for testing failed calibration
30. Laboratory records not maintained for prescribed period
31. Sample not refrigerated when not in transit
32. Sample not sealed and labeled as required by Ohio Department of Health
33. Chain of custody for sample not properly documented and retained
34. Sample not retained for additional testing
35. Laboratory did not successfully complete national proficiency testing program
36. Analyst did not have a valid laboratory technician or director permit
37. Laboratory report inadequate
38. Medical condition affected result of test
39. Medication affected result of test
40. Analyst error in testing sequence
41. Instrument used for testing has internal contamination
42. Balance instruments not calibrated
43. Internal standards, standards, and controls invalid
44. Uncertainty in measurement not calculated
45. Mass spectrometer spectral library used for confirmation invalid
46. Blood draw not conducted by qualified individual
47. Blood draw not conducted with sterile dry needle into vacuum container

48. Blood collected in container without solid anticoagulant
49. Urine sample not collected in accordance with Ohio regulations
50. Urine alcohol level at time of operating vehicle was below the 'legal limit' due to pooling of alcohol in urine

DEFENSES TO THE ADMINISTRATIVE LICENSE SUSPENSION

If you refuse a breath/blood/urine test or test 'over the limit', an Administrative License Suspension (ALS) is imposed by the Ohio Bureau of Motor Vehicles. When you are subjected to an ALS, you have the right to due process of law. That means the ALS is only valid if the officer followed the procedures required by Ohio law. That also means you must be given the opportunity to appeal the suspension.

The lawyers at the Dominy Law Firm created a list of defenses to the ALS called '*50 Ways to Leave Your ALS Lover*'. The defenses are asserted by filing a motion appealing the ALS and a separate motion to terminate the ALS.

Here are the top 10 defenses to the ALS:

1. Officer did not have reasonable grounds to believe driver was under the influence
2. Officer did not properly advise driver of consequences for taking or refusing a chemical test
3. Driver did not refuse a chemical test or test result was not 'over the limit'
4. Officer did not have a witness while reading the ALS form
5. Officer did not notify driver of the rights to appeal and independent chemical test
6. Officer completed the ALS report incorrectly

7. Officer did not give a complete ALS report to the driver
8. Officer did not have the ALS report sworn properly
9. Officer did not send the ALS report to the BMV, or the court, within 48 hours
10. Driver's initial appearance in court not held within five business days

The Administrative License Suspension is addressed at the first court appearance: the arraignment. The arraignment and the other stages of the court process are discussed in *Part Four*.

PART FOUR: THE COURT PROCESS FOR OVI CASES

ARRAIGNMENT

The first court appearance for an OVI case is the arraignment. The date and time of the arraignment is written by the officer at the bottom of the traffic ticket, and the arraignment should take place within five business days of the incident. At the arraignment, you will be given the choice of entering one of three pleas: (1) guilty; (2) no contest; or (3) not guilty.

You should give serious thought to what plea you will enter at the arraignment. Pleading *guilty* is a complete admission of your guilt, and the judge will enter a finding of guilty. Pleading *no contest* is an admission of the facts alleged in the ticket, and, if the ticket is correctly written, the judge will enter a finding of guilty. If you plead *guilty or no contest* at the arraignment, you will be sentenced, the case will be over, and you will not have the opportunity to defend yourself.

If you plead *not guilty* at the arraignment, you will have an opportunity to review the evidence against you, present evidence in your favor, and defend yourself against the accusation of OVI. Some people worry that pleading not guilty will lead to a harsher sentence if they later plead guilty or are later found guilty. Generally, that does not happen. Judges understand you must plead not guilty at the arraignment so you can at least review the evidence and evaluate the strength of the prosecution's case.

In addition to entering a plea at the arraignment, your attorney should address the Administrative License Suspension (ALS). As previously discussed, there are two ways to attack the ALS: a motion *appealing* the ALS, and a motion to *terminate* the ALS. Those motions should be filed at or before the arraignment.

If the judge does not hold a hearing on those motions at the arraignment, which often happens because the arraignment court is busy, the judge can issue a 'stay' of the ALS. If a stay is issued, your license is returned, so you can drive unrestricted until a full ALS hearing is held. If a stay is not issued, you can request limited driving privileges after the waiting period ('hard time') has elapsed.

What Plea should I Enter at the Arraignment?

The majority of people charged with OVI plead guilty at the arraignment. If you do that, there is a 100% chance you will be found guilty of OVI and have the OVI conviction on your record for the rest of your life. By pleading not guilty, you give yourself a chance of avoiding an OVI conviction. This question is addressed more thoroughly in the section of Part Four titled 'Should I Plead Guilty Or Fight It'?

DISCOVERY

Discovery is the process of exchanging evidence between the prosecution and defense. To initiate the discovery process, your attorney should file a *Demand For Discovery*. The information you receive in the discovery from the prosecution should include:

- the arrest report and narratives from the arresting officers
- witness statements and statements you made to the officer
- an alcohol/drug influence report and a report on field sobriety tests
- test results from blood/breath/urine tests and expert witness reports
- video from the police cruiser and body cameras
- an Administrative License Suspension report
- your criminal/traffic record

In addition to filing the *Demand For Discovery*, your attorney can obtain evidence through public records requests. Evidence which may be obtained through public records requests includes:

- video from the jail and/or police station
- maintenance records for the breath-testing machine
- breath-testing machine operator permits
- laboratory records for blood and urine tests
- permits for the laboratory technician and lab director
- 911 calls and communication among officers and dispatchers

If your case involves a blood or urine test, your attorney should file a *Demand for Testimony* of the laboratory technician who performed the blood or urine test. If this demand is not filed, the test report will be admitted as evidence without your attorney having the opportunity to cross-examine the laboratory technician.

When your attorney files a *Demand For Discovery*, there is an obligation to provide reciprocal discovery to the prosecution. The reciprocal discovery should include any of the following items that are relevant in your case: list of witnesses, witness statements, photographs, maps, videos, medical records, and expert witness reports.

The discovery process takes place primarily between the arraignment and the pretrial hearing. Most prosecutors' offices provide discovery in two parts. The first part is written materials, and the second part is video and audio recordings. Depending on what office is prosecuting your case, what law enforcement agency was involved, and the extent of the discovery materials, receiving discovery can take anywhere from a few days to a few weeks.

If you are represented by a lawyer, the discovery will be delivered by the prosecuting attorney to your lawyer. Your lawyer should then share the discovery with you. At the Dominy Law Firm, we share each piece of discovery electronically as we receive it. We then schedule meetings or phone conferences with the client to discuss the discovery, evaluate the case, and make recommendations.

Help Your Lawyer Help You

Soon after your arrest, while the incident is fresh in your mind, you should write a statement to give to your lawyer. The statement should include everything you can remember about the incident. You also should make a list of witnesses and their contact information. Even if there was nobody with you at the time of the stop, there may be individuals who saw you just before or after the stop and can confirm you were not under the influence. Another good thing to do is prepare a list of medical conditions and medications. Some of those cause symptoms that mimic intoxication or affect field sobriety tests or chemical tests.

PRETRIAL HEARING

The second court appearance is the pretrial hearing. In some courts, it's called a status conference, and in others it's called a discovery conference. Regardless of the name, the purpose of the pretrial is for the prosecution and defense to discuss the case and negotiate toward an agreed outcome (plea agreement, plea bargain). If you reach an agreement at the pretrial, you may go before the judge to finalize the agreement.

If you are serious about avoiding an OVI conviction, your case will probably not be finished at the pretrial. I once had a judge say, "Shawn, you don't have a track record of resolving cases at the pretrial", to which I replied, "That's because the prosecutors don't have a track record of making good offers at the pretrial."

It's true. At some pretrials, the prosecution has not reviewed or provided all the evidence. Even if the evidence has been reviewed and provided, the plea offer at the pretrial hearing often is not favorable for two reasons.

First, prosecutors prefer to have a conviction for the most serious offense charged on the ticket, so they offer a plea to that offense. For example, the prosecutor may dismiss the minor offense leading to the stop (Marked Lanes, Speeding, etc.) in exchange for a plea to the offense of OVI. If the defendant is willing to accept that, the prosecutor is very satisfied. The case is resolved without much work, and the prosecutor gets the conviction they want.

Second, if the plea offer is not accepted at the pretrial, it does not have an immediate effect the prosecutor. When the defendant rejects the plea offer, another hearing is scheduled, and the prosecutor is done with the case for that day. Prosecutors are typically dealing with many cases each day, so it is common for them to focus on the short-term goal of getting through the day's cases.

Unfortunately, many of the people who plead not guilty at the arraignment turn around and plead guilty to OVI at the pretrial. In most cases, to find out if the offer may get better, you need to go to the next stage of the case: the motion hearing.

Seven Steps for Evaluating Plea Offers

Deciding whether to accept an offer for a plea agreement cannot be reduced to a mathematical equation, but going through these seven steps will help you make the decision.

1. *What is the best-case scenario*? The best case scenario is a not guilty verdict or dismissal and no punishment.

2. *What is the likelihood of the best-case scenario?* Based on your attorney's thorough assessment of the prosecution's case, your defense, and the jurisdiction, predict the likelihood of obtaining a not guilty verdict. Naturally, this prediction is an art and not a science.

3. *What is the worst-case scenario?* A guilty verdict and the anticipated sentence that follows. Knowing the anticipated sentence requires familiarity with the judge's sentencing inclinations from prior cases, from reputation, or from representations made by the judge regarding this particular case.

4. *What is the likelihood of the worst-case scenario?* Because you and your attorney have assessed the strength of the case and predicted the likelihood of a not guilty verdict, you can also predict the likelihood of a guilty verdict. This evaluation is, of course, limited by the difficulty of predicting what verdict a jury will reach. It's more difficult in some cases than others.

5. *What is the certain scenario of the proposed agreement?* Assuming the agreement is approved by the judge, this is one factor in the evaluation that is known.

6. *Determine your risk tolerance.* Some clients are more risk averse than others.

7. *Analyze the factors in steps 3-6.* Compare the worst case scenario and its likelihood to the proposed settlement, taking into

account your risk tolerance. Determine if it's better to have the certain outcome of the proposed agreement or better to try for the best case scenario, taking into account the possibility of the worst case scenario.

MOTION HEARING

When evidence is suppressed, it is thrown out (excluded) and cannot be used at trial. Based on what your lawyer finds in the discovery, your lawyer should probably file motions to suppress evidence. Many specific motions may be filed, but most of them fall into one of these categories:

- Motions to suppress evidence based upon search and seizure law
- Motions to suppress evidence based upon the Rules of Evidence
- Motions to suppress field sobriety tests
- Motions to suppress breath/blood/urine tests
- Motions to suppress your statements

Your lawyer also should have filed a motion appealing the ALS and a motion to terminate the ALS. Although the ALS is first addressed at the arraignment, the hearing for the ALS is usually postponed and held at the same time as the hearing for the motions to suppress evidence.

At the motion hearing, just before the hearing starts, there is typically a last-minute negotiation. This stage of the case is often the first time the prosecution takes a close look at the evidence and engages in meaningful negotiations. This stage of the case is also the first time the prosecution's witnesses need to appear in court. If there is a significant chance that evidence will be suppressed, and/or if there is a significant chance that you may be found not guilty in a trial, the plea offer made at the pretrial often gets better. You usually need to get to this stage of the case to find out what is really the 'final offer'.

If you do not accept the prosecutor's offer, a motion hearing will be held. At the hearing, the officer(s) and any other prosecution witnesses will testify about what they observed and what they did. You or your attorney will have the opportunity to cross-examine the prosecution's witnesses, and you also may call defense witnesses. Each side then argues to the judge about what conclusions should be reached from the evidence. The judge issues a decision on the motions, either verbally (immediately following the hearing) or in writing (at a later time).

Motion hearings 'separate the men from the boys'. Although many lawyers have some understanding of the issues raised in motion hearings, few lawyers actually have extensive experience conducting motion hearings. Cross-examining witnesses and making legal arguments is an art, and one's mastery of that art improves with experience.

Just as you would not want your surgery to be your doctor's first, you do not want your motion hearing to be your attorney's first. You will want to find out which attorneys have experience and success in OVI motion hearings. The prosecutors know who those attorneys are. They also know which attorneys are just bluffing when they file motions to suppress.

At the Dominy Law Firm, we have experience and success with motion hearings. In every case, we conduct legal research, file motions to suppress, and prepare to litigate the motions. We enjoy motion hearings (and trials): cross-examining witnesses and making arguments is one of the best parts of practicing criminal defense. Another great part is helping clients avoid OVI convictions. That's why we do not represent clients who intend to plead guilty. We only represent clients who are pleading not guilty with the goal of improving the case outcome.

Case Example

Our client was pulled over for marked lanes. The officer smelled alcohol, so he administered field sobriety tests. The officer arrested our client, and our client's breath test result was .163, so our client was charged with OVI "per se" and OVI "impaired".We had a motion hearing on the admissibility of the breath test and the field sobriety tests. Cross examination revealed the police department did not comply with the regulations for maintaining the breath-testing machine, and the arresting officer did not comply with the protocol for administering sobriety tests. The judge suppressed the breath test and all three field sobriety tests. The prosecutor dismissed both charges of OVI – minutes before the jury trial was to begin.

TRIAL

If your case is not resolved at the motion hearing, it will be scheduled for a trial. You have the right to a trial, and you can choose to have a jury trial or bench trial. In a jury trial, a jury of eight people (12 for a felony) decides whether the prosecution proved your guilt. In a bench trial, a single judge makes that decision.

The trial has multiple parts. First is jury selection. After the jury is seated, each side gives an opening statement. The prosecution witnesses testify, the defense witnesses testify, and the prosecution may call rebuttal witnesses. Following the witness testimony, each side makes closing arguments. The jurors then retire to the jury room for jury deliberation (discussing the evidence) until they reach a unanimous decision. When the jury deliberates, they begin with the presumption you are not guilty. They can only render a guilty verdict if all the jurors agree the prosecution proved your guilt beyond a reasonable doubt.

Few OVI cases actually go to trial: fewer than five percent. In most cases, the prosecution and defense make similar predictions about the likely outcome of a trial, so they reach a plea agreement. The cases which do go to trial are often cases in which the prosecution and defense cannot reach an agreement because they have very different predictions about the likely outcome of the trial. Other cases go to trial because the prosecutor will not reduce charges, but the client absolutely cannot afford an OVI conviction and has nothing to lose by having a trial.

It is important to choose a defense lawyer with trial experience. Imagine you are taking a flight on a commercial airline. You ignore the flight attendant's presentation about safety, and you don't give any thought to the pilot's qualifications, because there are rarely problems with commercial flights. If there is a problem, however, you want a pilot with skill and experience flying the plane.

If you were charged with OVI, there is a problem, so you want a lawyer with skill and experience handling your case. That experience must include trials, and most lawyers have not taken many cases to trial. Prosecutors know which lawyers have trial experience and are therefore ready, willing, and able to take cases to trial.

Case Example: OVI 'Impaired'

Our client was pulled over for speeding and weaving, and the officer noticed the usual signs of intoxication: odor of alcohol, glassy/bloodshot eyes, and slurred speech. The officer administered field sobriety tests and arrested our client. Our client took the breath test, and the result was .113.

At the hearing on our motions to suppress, the evidence showed the police department did not comply with breath-testing regulations. Specifically, the police department failed to maintain records for the breath-testing machine as required by Ohio law. The judge suppressed the breath test, so it could not be mentioned during the trial.

At the trial, our theory was this: once the officer observed those usual signs of intoxication, he jumped to conclusions and only took into account evidence which supported his conclusion. Although an objective consideration of all the evidence may have led the officer to decide differently, he only saw the evidence pointing toward intoxication because 'the eye sees what the mind expects'. The jury apparently agreed with that theory, as they returned a quick verdict of Not Guilty.

Case Example: OVI 'Per Se

Our client was stopped for marked lanes and headlights violations, and the officer observed signs of intoxication. The officer administered field sobriety tests and arrested our client. Our client took a breath test, and the result was .069. The officer suspected our client had smoked marijuana, so the officer took a urine sample. The urine test showed no marijuana but indicated an alcohol level of .138. Our client was charged with OVI 'Impaired' and OVI 'Per Se', but the prosecutor elected to go forward only on the charge of OVI 'Per Se'.

At trial, we cross-examined the laboratory technician who administered the urine test. The lab tech admitted there are variables which can affect the test and make the result inaccurate. The lab tech also admitted the urine alcohol level may have been higher at the time of the sample than at the time of operating the vehicle because alcohol pools in the bladder. The jury returned a verdict of Not Guilty.

SENTENCING

If you plead guilty to something (OVI or a lesser offense), or if you are found guilty in a trial, the judge will hold a sentence hearing to determine what punishment to impose. The sentencing may be held on the same day as the guilty plea or trial, or it may be held separately, at a later date.

At the sentence hearing, the prosecutor may make a recommendation regarding the sentence, and your defense attorney will make a statement on your behalf. The judge will ask if there is anything you would like to say on your own behalf before the sentence is imposed. You are not required to make a statement. If you do make a statement, it should be concise.

After hearing from the prosecutor, the defense attorney, and you, the judge announces the sentence. Judges have wide latitude in what sentence to impose. For example, in a first-offense OVI, the judge can impose as little as three days in jail or as much as six months in jail. The judge will consider factors such as prior convictions, the result of the blood/breath/urine test, whether an accident and injury were involved, your attitude with police, and your acceptance of responsibility.

It may be beneficial to have a defense attorney speak on your behalf at the sentence hearing to effectively explain why the judge should exercise leniency in your case. Your attorney also should complete a form notifying the Bureau of Motor Vehicles of the outcome of the ALS appeal. Failure to complete this form may result in confusion about the length of your license suspension and complicate your driver license reinstatement.

Speaking at the Sentence Hearing

When the judge asks you what you want to say on your own behalf, the last thing the judge wants to hear is excuses. It usually is best to acknowledge you made a mistake, accept responsibility for your mistake, and indicate you will make efforts to avoid making that mistake in the future. It also is beneficial to express an understanding of the danger your conduct posed to others. Give thought to what you will say, but don't memorize a speech.

PART FIVE: MAKING DECISIONS ABOUT YOUR CASE

CAN OVI CASES REALLY BE WON?

Expectations about winning OVI cases vary greatly. Some people think, "If the officer concluded I was under the influence, or the test result was 'over the limit', there is nothing I can do to avoid an OVI conviction". Other people think, "No matter how bad the evidence is, if I hire a good lawyer, I will automatically avoid an OVI conviction". The truth is somewhere in-between.

Just because the officer says you were under the influence, or the test result was 'over the limit', does not mean you can't avoid an OVI conviction. I repeatedly see cases that seem strong for the prosecution at the beginning but turn out to be weak for the prosecution by the end. At the beginning of a case, there is no way to determine exactly how strong the case will be. To find out, you have to plead not guilty, investigate the evidence, and determine what evidence will be admissible in court. With the help of a skilled and experienced lawyer, contesting the OVI charge often results in the OVI charge getting reduced or amended to something other than OVI.

Case Example

Our client blew through a stop sign, squealed his tires as he sped away from the intersection, and took a long time to pull over after the cruiser lights came on. The officer observed the odor of alcohol, slurred speech, glassy/bloodshot eyes, and 'obvious intoxication'. Our client reportedly performed poorly on field sobriety tests, and our client's breath test result was .189.

The cruiser video showed the officer quickly concluded our client was drunk and shared that conclusion with the back-up officers even before getting our client out of the car for field sobriety tests. The officer ran through the field sobriety tests but just went through the motions and administered them poorly.

The records for the breath-testing machine showed a significant mistake in the maintenance of the machine. If the test result for the weekly instrument check is not what it should be, the check is supposed to be repeated with a different bottle of check solution. Rather than doing that, the police department repeated the check with the same bottle of check solution and did not change the bottle for a few weeks.

The breath test was going to be excluded, and the prosecution's case without it was questionable. As a result, the stop sign violation was dismissed, one OVI charge was dismissed, and the other OVI charge was amended to the non-moving violation of Physical Control, with no license suspension.

A case which seemed strong for the prosecution illustrates the point: *just because the officer says you were under the influence, or the test result is over the limit, does not mean you can't avoid an OVI conviction.*

On the other hand, just because you hire a good OVI lawyer does not guarantee that you will avoid an OVI conviction. A good OVI lawyer knows what to look for in the evidence and how to exploit weaknesses in the prosecution's case. There are instances, however, when there are no weaknesses in the case which lead to the OVI charge being reduced. A lawyer cannot file a motion to change the facts.

At the beginning of your case, you should define what is a 'win' for you. Some people may consider it a 'win' to get the most lenient sentence possible when pleading guilty to OVI. Others may only consider it a 'win' to have all of the charges dismissed or to be found not guilty of all the charges. A win for most people is in the middle: a win is avoiding an OVI conviction on your record. In the vast majority of cases handled by my firm, the OVI charge is reduced.

Once you define your win, you can address the remaining questions:

*Should I plead guilty or fight it?
*Should I hire a lawyer?
*Are all OVI lawyers the same?
*How do I choose a good OVI lawyer?

SHOULD I PLEAD GUILTY OR FIGHT IT?

To make this decision, you should consider what happens if you plead guilty, what happens if you plead not guilty, and whether it is worth the cost and time to fight the case and possibly avoid an OVI conviction.

If you plead guilty to the OVI, the judge will impose the sentence, and you will serve that sentence without ever reviewing the prosecution's evidence. You cannot change your mind later and decide you want to evaluate the strength of the prosecutor's case. There is a 100% chance that you will be convicted of OVI, and the conviction will be on your record forever.

If you plead not guilty to the OVI, you will have an opportunity to review the evidence against you. You will be able to evaluate the strength of the case and assert defense(s) to the charge(s). By contesting the case, you give yourself a chance of getting the OVI charge dismissed or reduced.

In many cases, the evidence against you is not as strong as it seems on the surface, and there is a good chance you can resolve the case without an OVI on your permanent record. An overwhelming majority of our clients avoid an OVI conviction.

Not everybody should contest their OVI charge. For some, the consequences of an OVI conviction are acceptable, or the cost of fighting it is too high. For others, it is worth the time and cost to try to avoid an OVI conviction.

Each person has to do their own cost-benefit analysis: is it worth paying the lawyer's fee for the probability you will avoid an OVI conviction. If you conclude it is not worth the money (or your time) to fight the OVI, you should plead guilty. If you want the opportunity to avoid an OVI conviction and you are willing to invest the time and money to fight it, you should plead not guilty.

SHOULD I HIRE A LAWYER?

To decide if you should hire a lawyer, you should evaluate how much you understand OVI issues, how familiar you are with court procedures, and how well you speak in public. You should also know whether you intend to contest the OVI or simply plead guilty.

If you intend to plead guilty to the OVI, you may not need a lawyer. If you feel comfortable with court appearances and speaking in public, you may be fine handling the case yourself. If not, hiring a lawyer can be worthwhile, even if you don't intend to fight the OVI. Like a tour guide in a foreign country, the lawyer can guide you through unfamiliar territory, explain what to expect, and warn you of dangers. The lawyer can also answer your questions, prepare court paperwork, and speak on your behalf at your hearing.

If you intend to contest the OVI, you should probably hire a lawyer. OVI lawyers are familiar with the Rules of Evidence, Rules of Criminal Procedure, Ohio Revised Code sections, Ohio Administrative Code sections, and cases interpreting all of those laws. Good OVI lawyers also have a firm understanding of field sobriety tests, blood/breath/urine tests, and drug recognition evaluations.

The lawyer must create a defense strategy, support it with motions to suppress, and communicate convincingly in negotiations with the prosecutor. An OVI lawyer must be accomplished in the art of examining witnesses, making arguments to a judge, and presenting a case to a jury. Given these demands, it is not impossible to represent yourself, but most people cannot do it effectively.

If you intend to contest the case, handling an OVI yourself is like treating your own medical problem. You can read about your medical problem on the internet (or at the library - remember those?), but if you need surgery, you should go to a doctor with expertise in that type of surgery. Likewise, you can read about OVI issues online, but if you are going to effectively contest the charge, you should go to a lawyer with expertise in OVI defense.

If you decide to hire a lawyer for your OVI, you are probably wondering if all lawyers are essentially the same.

ARE ALL OVI LAWYERS THE SAME?

If you are an NFL team owner, does it matter who plays quarterback for your team? Although all the NFL quarterbacks are good -they made it to the NFL- some are better than others. The same is true with lawyers. Although all lawyers made it through law school, some are better than others at OVI defense.

The skill of the quarterback matters so much that Kansas City Chiefs quarterback Patrick Mahomes is paid $45 million per year while (former Buckeye) Dwayne Haskins of the Pittsburgh Steelers is paid only $850,000 per year (how can he survive on that?!). If you are facing an OVI, the skill of your lawyer matters too.

To be skilled at OVI defense, a lawyer must be proactive: most law schools do not teach OVI defense. To achieve expertise in defending clients charged with OVI, a lawyer should start with independently reading all the relevant court decisions related to OVI law, as well as all the statutes, rules and regulations. Next, the lawyer should learn about police procedures, forensics, field sobriety testing, breath testing, blood and urine testing, psychology, sociology, persuasion, and litigation. Finally, the lawyer needs to put that knowledge to use in court by litigating motion hearings and jury trials.

As you can see, there is a lot to learn and experience to be a good OVI lawyer. It is practically impossible to develop expertise in OVI while practicing other areas of law. For this reason, it is generally not a good idea to be represented for OVI by the family friend who handles divorces or business transactions but is willing to 'help out' with your OVI. Just as you would not go to your general practice doctor for brain surgery, you should not go to a general practice lawyer for OVI defense.

Many lawyers talk about doing what's necessary to develop expertise, but few actually do it. In Central Ohio, there are only a handful of lawyers who have developed expertise in OVI defense. Those attorneys get better results for their clients. The lawyers who don't put in the work to develop expertise often commit the 'seven deadly sins' of OVI defense.

The 'Seven Deadly Sins' of OVI Defense

1. *Limiting the attack on the Administrative License Suspension (ALS).* There are two ways to attack the ALS: (a) a motion *appealing* of the ALS, and (b) a motion to *terminate* the ALS. Most lawyers file an appeal but do not file a motion to terminate. That is a mistake because there are many technicalities that can get the ALS terminated, and those technicalities are not addressed in an ALS appeal.

2. *Failing to timely file motions to suppress evidence.* If the lawyer does not file motions to suppress evidence by the deadline, all the prosecution's evidence will be admissible. If the lawyer files the motions by the deadline, the lawyer gives you a chance of getting evidence excluded.

3. *Inadequately challenging the field sobriety tests (FSTs).* The lawyer should file a motion to suppress the FSTs, and the lawyer should go through the same FST training as officers to challenge the tests effectively. Most lawyers do not go through the training and are therefore less likely to recognize when officers make mistakes administering the tests.

4. *Ignoring the multiple phases of an OVI investigation.* An OVI investigation has several phases and involves more than just the FSTs. By completing the same training as officers for OVI investigations, a lawyer can identify when officers do not follow protocol and when evidence does not support the officer's conclusion the driver was under the influence.

5. *Assuming the rules were followed for chemical tests.* To determine whether the government complied with state regulations to make the blood/breath/urine test admissible, the lawyer needs to review law enforcement records that are not provided in the discovery process. Sadly, few attorneys review these records.

6. *Giving up too early.* Most lawyers plead their clients guilty at the arraignment or pretrial, so they never find out if the offer would have gotten better by reaching the next stage of the case: the motion hearing.

7. *Taking on too many cases*. Many lawyers who advertise themselves as 'DUI lawyers' handle a high volume of cases (usually for a low fee) and spend little time on each case. Those are the lawyers who plead their clients guilty at the arraignment or pretrial without doing all the work necessary to put their clients in a position to avoid an OVI conviction.

HOW DO I CHOOSE A GOOD OVI LAWYER?

If you have a serious medical condition, the likelihood of overcoming the condition increases if you are treated by a good doctor with expertise in that condition. If you are charged with OVI, the likelihood of avoiding an OVI conviction increases if you are represented by a good lawyer with expertise in OVI. The following tools will assist you in finding a good OVI lawyer:

- Resources for researching lawyers
- 10 traits to look for in an OVI lawyer
- 11 questions to ask about an OVI lawyer's practice
- 12 questions to ask about an OVI lawyer's qualifications

RESOURCES FOR RESEARCHING LAWYERS

Ohio Supreme Court: Every attorney in the state of Ohio is required to register with the Ohio Supreme Court. You can verify that a prospective attorney currently is licensed to practice in Ohio, and you can determine if the attorney has been disciplined by conducting an attorney information search.

Avvo.com: Avvo® is a website designed to help consumers research attorneys. The site contains profiles of most attorneys in Ohio, and each attorney is given a rating between 1.0 and 10.0. The profile contains the attorney's resume and also includes client reviews and peer endorsements. You can search for attorneys by practice area and geographic area on the page titled 'Find A Lawyer'.

Lawyer Directory Websites: There are many websites which have lawyer directories. Some of them are for all types of lawyers, and some of them are for OVI lawyers. Most directories are not very valuable because they do not really tell you objectively who the best lawyers are. The exceptions are: Super Lawyers®, Martindale-Hubbell®, and Best Lawyers in America®.

10 TRAITS TO LOOK FOR IN AN OVI LAWYER

1. *Focus*. Choose a lawyer whose practice is focused on OVI defense. There are hundreds of lawyers who will represent you for an OVI case in central Ohio. Most of them, however, also practice other areas of law. If you were having foot surgery, would you hire a family doctor with a general practice, or would you hire a foot surgeon?

2. *Expertise*. Select a lawyer with expertise in OVI defense. Many lawyers know the basics of OVI defense, but few have a deeper understanding of the issues in these cases. Most lawyers with expertise in OVI defense are members of the National College for DUI Defense (NCDD).

3. *Experience*. It is necessary to have knowledge and expertise, but it's also important to have experience. Just as you do not want your surgery to be your doctor's first, you do not want your OVI case to be the first one in which your lawyer argues a motion to suppress evidence or presents a case to a jury. Hire a lawyer with both expertise and experience.

4. *Service*. Choose a lawyer who provides good customer service. The number one complaint about lawyers is they do not communicate well with their clients. Your lawyer should keep you updated regarding all developments in your case, provide you with documents related to your case, and answer all of your questions. You can expect better service from a lawyer who accepts fewer cases rather than a lawyer with a high-volume practice.

5. *Personality*. You should find a lawyer with good people skills. If your lawyer does not interact well with you, how is he or she going to interact with the prosecuting attorney, the judge, and the jury when advocating for you?

6. *Industry recognition*. Select a lawyer who is recognized by his or her peers as a leader in OVI defense. Those lawyers often are asked to teach other lawyers about OVI at continuing education seminars. Those lawyers are also often selected for Super Lawyers® and Best Lawyers in America®. In addition, peer reviews are

available on Avvo.com.

7. *No guarantees*. In nearly all OVI cases, it is impossible for a lawyer to predict with certainty what will be the outcome of your case. To properly evaluate a case, a lawyer must review all the evidence, relevant law, and many other factors. All the evidence in a case will not be known until discovery is exchanged and an investigation is completed. Do not hire a lawyer who guarantees a certain outcome in your initial consultation.

8. *Results*. Choose a lawyer who has a history of obtaining good results for clients. A lawyer should be willing to publish, or at least share with you, the results of cases similar to yours. Hire a lawyer that has a proven record of results.

9. *Client satisfaction*. Find a lawyer who has satisfied clients. Client testimonials are available on many lawyers' websites. An even better source, Avvo.com, is an independent third party that collects reviews from clients and rates lawyers. Hire a lawyer with high ratings from previous clients.

10. *Appropriate fees*. Select a lawyer who charges appropriate fees. You can find inexpensive representation, but a lawyer who charges low fees in OVI matters either does not intend to do all the work necessary to present a good defense or does not have the expertise and experience to get good results. A low fee may also indicate what the lawyer thinks about the value of his or her service.

Remember the discussion of quarterbacks Patrick Mahomes and Dwayne Haskins? They both provide the same service, playing quarterback, but Patrick Mahomes is paid 50 times as much as Dwayne Haskins because Mahomes has a proven record of good results. A lawyer with expertise and a proven record of good results is going to charge higher fees than a lawyer without the same expertise and results.

11 QUESTIONS TO ASK ABOUT AN OVI LAWY'ER PRACTICE

1. Where did you go to law school, how long have you been practicing?
2. Please give me an overview of your career.
3. Have you ever been disciplined as an attorney?
4. To what professional organizations do you belong?
5. How many OVI cases have you handled?
6. How many new clients do you accept each month?
7. How many cases do you have pending currently?
8. How do you communicate with your clients and how frequently?
9. Will you provide me with everything you receive and file for my case?
10. Where can I read reviews about you, other than your website?
11. How much is your fee and what does it include?

12 QUESTIONS TO ASK ABOUT AN OVI LAWYER'S QUALIFICATIONS

1. What percentage of your practice is OVI defense?
2. Are you a member of the National College for DUI defense?
3. What do you do to improve your skills as an OVI lawyer?
4. Are you ever asked to teach other lawyers about OVI?
5. What are the relevant laws and manuals for field sobriety testing?
6. How do the breath-testing machines in Ohio work?
7. What is your strategy for challenging breath/blood/urine tests?
8. What role does search and seizure law play in OVI cases?
9. What role does *Miranda* play in OVI cases?
10. How will you contest the Administrative License Suspension?
11. How many times have you cross-examined officers in OVI cases?
12. What percentage of your clients charged with OVI plead guilty at the arraignment or the pretrial?

CONCLUSION

You made a great decision to read this guide. Unlike most people charged with OVI, you are not in the dark. You now have the information you need before going to court. You understand OVI charges, and you are aware of the possible consequences. You are familiar with the evidence in OVIcases and the possible defenses. You also know what to expect in the court process.

This guide has the information you need before making decisions about your OVI case. You have a framework to help you decide if you are going to fight the OVI and a guide for deciding whether you want a lawyer. If you choose to hire a lawyer, you have resources for researching lawyers, criteria to evaluate their qualifications, and questions to ask when you speak with them.

Don't be the victim of a 'DUI Lawyer' who takes your money and provides ineffective representation. There are only a handful of lawyers in central Ohio who have the expertise, experience, and other qualifications discussed in this guide.

Use the resources in this guide, do the research, and don't be afraid to ask questions. You will make well-reasoned decisions about how to handle your OVI case, and you will find a lawyer with the qualifications to improve the outcome.

ABOUT THE AUTHOR

Shawn Dominy

I have practiced OVI defense and criminal defense since 1997. In 2002, I began proactively developing expertise in OVI defense. I joined the National College for DUI Defense and completed specialized training in areas such as field sobriety testing, breath testing, and blood/urine testing. I also purchased the breath-testing machine used by most Ohio police departments so I could experiment with it.

The more I learned about OVI defense, the more I liked it. I continued with specialized training and gained extensive experience by taking hundred of cases through contested motion hearings and jury trials. I now teach lawyers about OVI and trial skills at state and national seminars, and my OVI articles have been featured in state and national publications. I am listed in Best Lawyers in America® for OVI defense and named by Super Lawyers® as one of the top 50 lawyers in Columbus.

My firm limits the number of cases we accept so we can work each case thoroughly and give every client the service and attention we would want as a client. We only represent clients in Central Ohio courts (Franklin County, Delaware County, and their contiguous counties), and we only represent clients contesting the OVI.

Based on our expertise, our experience, and the level of service we provide, my firm's fees are often higher than the fees charged by other attorneys. We offer flat fees, so clients know the exact amount of the fees up front.

You can learn more about OVI and my law firm on our website and our blog. If you finish your research and would like to discuss representation, you can schedule a free phone consultation by email or by calling the Dominy Law Firm at 614-717-1177.

PRAISE FOR AUTHOR

"This book is not only a must read for Ohio drivers charged with DUI, but also for Ohio lawyers wanting to provide quick and accurate information to their clients in urgent situations."

- NICHOLAS I. ANDERSEN, ESQ., ARENSTEIN & ANDERSEN CO., LPA

"Attorney Shawn Dominy takes complex information and breaks it down so the average citizen can digest it and use it to make wise choices in their DUI case. Attorney Dominy provides enlightening real-life case examples of how he has addressed various legal issues in the past and what to look for in your case. A must-read for those charged with DUI and new attorneys."

- ROBERT CALESARIC, ATTORNEY AT LAW

"Shawn's Ohio DUI / OVI Guide is genuinely invaluable. For someone facing a DUI/OVI charge, it concisely sets forth what to expect. As important, reading the book will elevate the reader's understanding of the various complexities involved in defending a DUI/OVI case. Knowing what lies ahead – the numerous court processes, the opportunities for a successful defense, the pitfalls to avoid, etc. – will make coping with the inherent stress of being charged more bearable. This book thoughtfully illustrates that the myriad of options and possibilities starts with

making the right choice in choosing your DUI/OVI defense attorney. Shawn's book should be required reading by everyone charged with a DUI/OVI."

-MARK GARDNER, ATTORNEY AT LAW

"The Ohio DUI / OVI Guide is a comprehensive and easily understandable resource to give those accused of OVI a thorough understanding of what to expect from the roadside investigation all the way through trial and sentencing. Shawn Dominy is recognized throughout Ohio as one of the leading authorities on OVI defense and is a regular speaker at the Advanced OVI Defense Seminar every spring - he teaches lawyers how to fight OVI charges. Mr. Dominy also provides some great tips on what to look for when shopping for an OVI lawyer; but the fact is, anyone charged with OVI would be well served by hiring Mr. Dominy. In conclusion, this is a great read and an excellent value."

-JEFFREY C. MEADOWS, ATTORNEY AT LAW

Made in the USA
Monee, IL
04 November 2026

67376404R00049